Success Filled Living

by
Shirley Thomas

Success Filled Living
by Shirley Thomas

Printed in the United States of America

ISBN 978-1-60266-749-5

www.xulonpress.com

Shirley Thomas
Success Filled Living
P.O. Box 77066
Washington, DC 20013
1-800-359-8336 X4052
shirley@shirleythomas.tv
successfilledliving.com

Acknowledgments

Of course, all the glory and all the honor goes to the Lord Jesus Christ. He is the one who empowers and enables us to do all that we do. I remember so often times down through the years, He would say, I don't mind blessing My children, Shirley. All I ask is that they remember to put me in remembrance. I am putting you in remembrance. Thank you, Lord Jesus.

Special thanks to Lynnmarie
for her wonderful suggestions
regarding the preparation of this book.

TABLE OF CONTENTS

Introduction

Down through the years, I have noticed time and time again how the world takes godly concepts, puts them in plain English, taking out the "thees" and "thous"; teach its principles and become financially wealthy. They live great lives. It looks like they never worry about not having enough of what they need to sustain themselves and they enjoy the things God created. But, the most important thing they need, they leave out; which is, "the Almighty God through His Son, Jesus".

Well, the scripture tells us that the Lord made everything for us to enjoy. But, here we are as Christians, we have Jesus. Yet, many Christians are not experiencing that kind of abundance, wealth, prosperity and enjoyment. Some are not living the Kingship or Kingdom life that was given to us to live. There is usually lack, poverty, scarcity, sickness and dis-ease going on in the believers' lives.

I have listened to motivational speakers down through the years, conducting seminars about positive thinking, "if you can believe, you can achieve, if your mind can conceive it, you can have it", etc. The world takes these thoughts and runs with them. They apply them to their lives and, nothing seemingly is impossible to them.

I want to let you in on a little secret. There are some parts of the Bible that will work even for a person that does not profess to know God if they apply those principles to their lives. Why? Because they are divine laws. Work the law and it has to come to pass. For example, give and it shall be given to you. It's a divine law. It has to work because the Bible didn't say, it was limited to "believers" give and it shall be given to you.

So, I started to seriously think about some things. There are some things in my life I have accomplished. There are some things in my life that have yet to come to pass. I knew that correct confession played a key part in my possessing. I have always been a person that adamantly believes in watching what I say. Ninety-nine percent of the time I would not say anything negative. When I did catch myself saying things that had no life in them, I would immediately retract those words and change my confession. But I finally realized where I was missing it. I was saying the right things, but I was thinking the wrong things. My thinking needed to line up with my saying.

That's why I am writing this book. This is where the Body of Christ has missed it. It is our thinking. We have been thinking the wrong things.

Through the pages of this book, you will come to understand how powerful your thinking plays in your obtaining your life-long dreams and aspirations. You will learn what to do to change. Through these pages you will come to another level of understanding of how profound, yet simple, God has made the Word of God when it comes to Him wanting us to understand how badly He wants us to live life to the fullest. Through these pages will <u>come a stirring</u> of your pure mind to grasp truths that have been there all the time yet maybe have been overlooked. How often have we said during our Christian walk, "I read that scripture many times before, but I never saw it like that". Through these pages the revelation of God's Word will be imparted into your spirit. Thoughts and scriptures that you have seen and heard over and over again will bring new light to you.

These words will be so refreshing to your soul as you discover, even the more, the power that lies within you to bring you to the fulfillment of your destiny. Get ready for mind provoking thoughts that, if implemented, will change your life forever.

But remember this won't occur without a battle, for this will be a battle for your thought life. But, also, remember the good thing is, that the battle is not yours; it's the Lord's. Therefore, you don't ever have to do anything all by yourself. You always have the power of the Holy Spirit to assist you in bringing every thought captive to the obedience of Jesus Christ. Simply, ask Him for His assistance. You are co-laborers with the Lord Jesus Christ. Take Him as a partner in everything you do and controlling your thoughts will become easier. Success Filled Living will be your portion.

Here are just a few scriptures validating the authenticity of the Word of God saying that we are to experience Success Filled Living in every area of our lives be it spiritually, physically, financially and emotionally.

Always remember that it is the Lord your God who gives you power to become rich and He does it to fulfill the covenant He made with your forefathers. Deut. 8:18

And it is a good thing to receive wealth from God and the good health to enjoy it. To enjoy your work and accept your lot in life – that is indeed a gift from God. People who do, they rarely look with sorrow on the past, for God has given them reasons for joy. Eccl: 5:19-20 (New Living Translation)

And I will give you the treasures of darkness and hidden riches of secret places. Isaiah 45:3 (Amplified Bible)

Success Filled Living. Um, that's interesting. Are you living the kind of Success Filled Life that you would like to live? Well, let me ask you another question? Exactly what does success mean? The dictionary defines success as, the achievement of something desired or attempted; the gaining of fame or prosperity. It definitely could mean one thing to one person and another thing to another person. But one thing I do know for sure, God wants you to have a successful, happy, blessed, and fulfilled life.

Chapter I
God Has Given Us Everything We Could Ever Want

It is my heart's desire to see God's people live the God kind of life that is spoken of in the Bible. So much was given for us as believers; the shed blood of Jesus Christ. Jesus was born of a virgin, died a death of crucifixion on the Cross and rose from the grave triumphantly three days later for you and me. Through the shedding of His blood, our sins have been forgiven. Our names have been written in the Lambs Book of Life. Jesus became our poverty so that we could receive His wealth. He took the road of death so that we could receive eternal life. He bore our sicknesses so that we could receive health. **We have now been given everything we could ever want**.

The scripture says, God has given you all things that pertain to life and godliness. (II Peter 1:3) God has given you everything you could ever want: joy, health, wealth, deliverance from disease, spiritual death and eternal damnation. Jesus paid for it all on the Cross.

Take a look at these scriptures. *Whatsoever things you desire when you pray, believe you have received them and you shall have whatsoever you ask for in prayer, (if you don't doubt) (Mark 11:24).*

And whatever you ask in prayer, having faith and really believing you will receive (Mat 21:22) Amplified.

Ask, and you shall receive so that your joy may be full, complete and overflowing.

Beloved, I wish above all things that thou mayest prosper and be in health even as thy soul prospereth (III John 3:2).

It sounds like to me you can have, do or be anything you want, as long as it doesn't violate the laws of God and harm your fellow man. For it is God who says, *I am able to do exceedingly above anything you could ask, imagine, think or even dream of (Eph. 3:20).* So, God will do for you and through you far above anything you could ever desire or even dream of. God says, to you and *I, that we can do all things through Christ that strengthens us (Phil 4:13)*. So, it sounds like, God will give us the strength and supernatural ability through His Son, Jesus, to do and accomplish anything we desire or anything we could ever dream of.

Do you have any dreams and aspirations? What do you want out of life? Do you want to be a millionaire? Go into your own business for yourself, live in a bigger house? What do you really desire? Miracles can take place in your life if you would just believe. It's very simple. It's in the Bible. You simply have to know how to appropriate the Word of God. Everything that comes to you in life, it comes to you, thru your mind.

You bring into your life that which you think about the most. It's a divine law: *So as man thinketh, so is he (Prov. 23:7). Man becomes what he thinks about the most.*

So, you are probably asking yourself, "Why haven't things come to pass in my life yet? I have been saying and doing all the right things. The problem is "our thinking has been off". You must start to think the right things. You must begin to think prosperous, healthy, and wealthy thoughts in your every wakening moment. In your mind you have about 30 to 60,000 thoughts a day. The majority are not life giving. You must turn those thoughts into life-giving, joyful, thoughts; thoughts that builds and edify. How? By thinking, I am healthy. I am wealthy. I am wise. I am anointed. I am empowered. I am more than a conqueror. I am a winner. I am an accomplisher and a finisher. I am in my wealthy place. I have tapped into the inheritance that Jesus died for me to have. I go into the storehouse of blessings and I receive in the Name of Jesus every package that has my name on it. I receive all good to me in Jesus name.

You are the only person in this world that can control your thinking. Others may influence or suggest, but only you can control what your mind accepts or rejects. You have to make a conscious effort to replace negative, self-defeating thoughts with faith filled, positive, fulfilling thoughts. It is a process that must be done every moment of the day until it becomes a part of you like a part of your skin on your body. Your mind will become stronger when you learn to do this. The secret is "control". You must exercise that control. The Bible says that *the Lord has not given us the spirit of fear, but of power, love and a sound mind*. In another translation, it says, *God has not given us the spirit of fear, but of power, love and a sane mind*. A sane mind is a controlled mind.

People, who have obtained any degree of success or wealth, don't allow uncontrolled, contradictory thoughts to take root in their minds. They constantly think thoughts of abundance, wealth, and happiness. The scripture tell us, *Finally, my brethren, whatsoever things are true, whatsoever things are honest, whatsoever things are just, whatsoever things are pure, whatsoever things are lovely, whatsoever things are of good report, if there be any virtue, if there be any praise, think on these things (Phil 4:8).* Notice in that scripture, whatsoever is repeated over and over again. I have found that when God feels the need to have something repeated in His Word, it is for a reason. The scripture could have said, whatsoever things are true, honest, just…. God is trying to get our attention here. He is trying to get us to really think on how important it is for us to think the right things. He is saying to us that this is serious business. Pay attention. Take heed. In one other place in the Bible, it tells us to take earnest heed and to not let these things slip. Don't allow thoughts that are contrary to the scriptures to filtrate your mind. When they come, rebuke them and start thinking faith-filled, positive thoughts again. Take a look at the above scripture again, *whatsoever things are true, whatsoever things are honest, whatsoever things are just, whatsoever things are pure, whatsoever things are lovely, whatsoever things are of good report*…. This is another scripture that the world has taken and achieved wealth. Where do you think the phrase "positive thinking" came from; or the title of the book, "Think and Grow Rich". Billions of dollars have made by the world system while we as Christians let the devil make us think, positive thinking is of him when it originated from the Word of God.

You have *the greatest power ever known living inside of you. It is the same power that raised Jesus Christ from the dead (Romans 8:11).* It is the same power that quickens your mortal body and is going to cause you to be *caught up in a moment in a twinkling of an eye when the trumpet blows and Jesus cracks the sky (I Cor 15:52),* to take the church home. It is more powerful than anything in the world. That power is sent out or released through your thoughts. You are drawing to you whatever you are thinking about over a long period of time. Have you ever said to yourself, "I wish she would sit down"? And then next thing you know, she sat down. Have you ever thought on something and next thing you know, there it was. Thoughts become things. Your thoughts or your prayers shall I say, were answered. You are bringing into your life the thing(s) you are thinking.

In the Christian arena, we don't say, I think it is so, after we have prayed for something and now waiting for its mani-festation. What we say is, I believe it is so. Because to say, I think it is so; to us sounds like unbelief. But that is not what I am saying to do here. What I am saying is, think, think, and think wealthy, healthy thoughts. Think good things coming into your life and you create that kind of world for yourself. You become what you think about the most.

What have been your dominant thoughts lately? Think about it. Are you thinking happiness, goodness, wealth, good health, and success? I have noticed especially when attending church, many of us, if we are not watchful, think about Sister Susie didn't speak to me today. Did you see that dress Judy had on? Oh, girl the spirit of the world is coming into the church. Women are wearing clothes with their breast out or short blouses showing their mid waist. Well, we should show moderation in how we dress. We should cover ourselves, especially since we name the name of the Lord Jesus Christ and we are ministers of the Gospel. But, what do you think we are creating? We definitely are not creating a desire to win souls nor to have wealth, health, peace, and prosperity. Why not channel all that energy to thinking, I will witness to three souls a week. I will lead one soul a week to Jesus. I am financially independent. I am a money missionary. I fund the gospel with my wealth, instead of thoughts of animosity, being judgmental, jealously, strife, etc. Why not think on the Fruit of the Spirit, which is love, joy, peace, longsuffering, gentleness, goodness, faith, meekness, and temperance. Think of confessions such as I am a loving person. I am a joyful person. I am a peacemaker. I am patient and gentle. I operate in goodness, faith and meekness and I am temperate in all my ways. These are the kind of thoughts we should be thinking. This is how you live and walk in the Spirit as we have been commanded to do. Think on, I live in my dream house. I drive my dream car. I am in my wealthy place. I live in abundance. I think prosperous thoughts.

The vibration of mental thoughts is one of the most powerful forces in the world. If you think you can, you can. If you think you can't, guess what? You can't. You know that you are at your best when you are concentrated and/or when you are having periods of intense thinking. See yourself in abundance, wealthy and healthy. In other words, focus. As you see yourself this way, you will begin to carry yourself differently. You will straighten up your shoulders and walk with more confidence. Carry yourself as if you already have abundance instead of seeing lack, scarcity, poverty and dis-ease. As you begin to think perfect things, you will begin to create perfect things and draw perfect things to yourself.

Chapter II
Something Else to Think About

Oh, but I know how believers think. I am one, too, remember. The first thing we are going to say is, **I am not going to think about anything more than God**. Okay, then, let's put God in it. Let's make it a time of worship. I thank you Heavenly Father that I am in my wealthy place. I worship you Holy Spirit for being my Comforter, Counselor, Teacher, Keeper, Best Friend, Lover and Confidant. I thank you Father God for I am whole, complete and lacking nothing. I thank you that I am Fathered and Counseled by You. You have informed me that I am prosperous and I have life more abundantly. Therefore, I move, live and have my being in that abundance. Don't take God out of it; include

Him in. Oh, He loves this. This is what He sent His Son Jesus to die for. He died so that He could fellowship with you and you with Him. He wants to be included in every aspect of your life. Now that you are including Him in with controlling your thinking, and creating your world, you can't help but have prosperity, joy, answered prayers, abundance, wealth, and divine health take place in your life. Think prosperity. Think health and wellness.

Tell God the amount of money you want in your bank account and then make it a worship. Christians would say, "I don't want to think like that". Why not? Who is going to fund the gospel, if not you and me? So, your thoughts are, Lord, I thank you that I have millions in my hands so that your Kingdom can be established. Make it a time of worship. Even when you are worshiping, you have to think something. I worship and praise you Heavenly Father that I have $$$$$$$$$ in my bank account. He will do it just because you ask *so that your joy may be full, complete and overflowing.*

Become aware of your thoughts and make a conscious effort to guard them. The Bible says, *for the weapons* (what could be a weapon – our right thinking) *of our warfare are not carnal, but mighty through God to the pulling down of*

strong holds, casting down imaginations (wrong thinking) and
every high thing that exalteth itself against the knowledge of
God, bringing into captivity every thought to the obedience
of Jesus Christ (II Cor. 10:5). What are strongholds? Our
dominant, adamant thoughts or thinking that does not line
up with the Word of God. What is the knowledge of God?
I'll tell you what it is not. If your thought is, I am suppose
to be poor, sick and defeated because I'm suffering for the
Lord. That thought is exalting itself against what God has
said in His Word and that is not His Knowledge. To know
that He doesn't want you sick, poor, busted and disgusted
is His Knowledge. Every thought we send out returns to the
source it came from which is God in you (if it is a good one
now). Think on good things.

God gave us a mind to imagine with. So if you are thinking
on something over and over and over and over again, you are
creating it, be it negative or positive. So why not imagine
driving that brand new car paid for. Living in that brand new
house built from the ground paid for. Seeing your soul mate
appear and that you and he/she are a ministry flourishing
in the Kingdom of God. Imagine that successful business,
career, etc. When you imagine these things on a consistent
basis, you are creating the power for them to come to pass.

Chapter III
Mind, Heart, Meditations

The Book of Romans, *tells us to be transformed by the renewing of our mind (through and by the Word of God) so that, we may prove what is that good and acceptable will of God (Romans 12:1). The New Living Translation Bible says it like this;* **Let God transform you into a new person by changing the way you think. Then you will know what God wants you to do and you will know how good and pleasing and perfect His will really is.** His will is that you prosper and be in health even as your soul prospers. His will is that you live life to the fullest. His will is that you have life and have it more abundantly. How do you get your soul to prosper? By thinking and meditating, and doing the living

Word of God. Start repeating over and over and over and over in your mind, my soul prospers, therefore, I prosper. Jesus takes pleasure in the prosperity of his servants/children and I am a child of the Most High God. Therefore, I am in my wealthy place. The Lord daily loads me with benefits. Therefore, I am healthy, wealthy and wise. I am empowered with the blessing by the Blessor. I have the mind of Christ. Therefore, I think on abundance. I think on wealth. I think on good health. I think on all my needs are met according to His Riches in Glory. I am a money missionary. You see, you are creating while you are thinking.

Mind, thoughts, thinking. Why are these so powerful, so prevalent, and so important? God wants your mind, your thoughts, your thinking. The devil wants your mind, your thoughts, your thinking. The Lord wants control of your mind and Satan wants control of your mind. The positive, faith filled thoughts come from God and the negative thoughts come from the devil. The devil wants to bombard you with so many negative thoughts that he wants you to become hopeless, helpless, frustrated to the point that you go do something crazy, like go shoot up everybody in the house and turn the gun on yourself, too. For example, you had a dispute on the job. You didn't get that promotion that maybe you so rightfully deserved. You go to the job, kill everybody and yourself, too. Or, the devil wants you to feel so hopeless regarding any particular situation that you commit suicide. It all starts with a thought in the mind. No, you have control over your thoughts. God wants you to mediate upon good things, things that build and edify and that are of good report. It is all about the mind. What the mind can conceive, it can achieve, be it good or evil. That is why in the Bible, in the story of Babel, the Lord came down and confounded their native tongue. They purposed in their heart to build a tower to reach heaven. The Lord said, they have one mind and will achieve this thing, less I go down and intervene. The mind is a very powerful apparatus. Use it for the Glory of God and use it to have a good, Success Filled Life.

These are the things we are usually thinking. I don't have enough money to pay the electric bill. My daughter is on drugs. The doctor said I had cancer. The boss gave me a pink slip today, and so on, and so on. These are things you don't want and guess what? That is what is showing up in your life, more of what you don't want, bills and challenges. Yes, the circumstances are real but only temporary if you can believe. Yes, you got a pink slip on the job today. Your daughter is on drugs. The report from the doctor was not good. But, don't dwell on it. Put your petition(s) before the Lord casting all your cares upon Him for He careths for you and He will perfect those things that concerns you. Then dwell on the answer you asked God for. By your stripes I am healed, Lord. One door closes another one opens, God. Therefore, I thank you for my new job. My daughter is saved, sanctified and filled with the Holy Ghost, Lord. She is delivered. Let these be your thoughts. Monitor what you are thinking on a daily basis. If it does not line up with the Word of God, change your thinking. Job said, *the very thing I greatly feared has come upon me (Job 3:25)*. Or the very thing I thought on with a lot of passion. When it comes to your thoughts, it doesn't matter whether they are good or bad; you are creating everything around you.

There is no such thing as an impossible situation. Every circumstance of your life can change if you change your mindset. Begin to consciously change the way you think and change your life.

Don't be alarmed by the negative thoughts you have had in the past. Start thinking positive, faith filled things because an affirmative thought has much more power than a negative one. Not all thoughts come to pass immediately. So, you have time to retract the negative ones and put them under the blood of Jesus. Start thinking, "all my good thoughts are powerful". All good things come to me. All negative thoughts are under the blood of Jesus and I render them null and void now. Time serves you. Start thinking good thoughts now and say to yourself, "I am the master of my thoughts."

Have you heard of the old saying "what ever will be, will be"? Well, if you believe that? Then, yes. That's a seed you are sowing and yes, that's what you will reap. But it doesn't have to be that way. You have a choice in the matter. God made you a free moral agent. *He set before you everyday, life and death, blessings and curses. Choose which one you may serve (Deut. 30:19).* It depends upon your thoughts, which become your actions. You control your destiny. You can believe that only good comes to me in my life, by thinking only good comes to me in my life and my family's lives. Now when something bad tries to show up to hurt you or your family, *God has given you power over all the works of the enemy that nothing by any means shall hurt you.* In other words, Jesus has given you the authority to use His name. Therefore, exercise that authority by binding and loosing. (*Whatever I bind on earth shall be bound in heaven (Mat 18:18). Whatever I loose on earth shall be loosed in heaven*). Then re-direct your thoughts/meditations regarding that situation. Praising God is one of the most powerful ways to re-direct your thoughts. You can't praise God and think on hurtful things at the same time.

By becoming strongly aware of your thoughts, the creative power within you will begin to work on your behalf to give you a phenomenal life. So, monitor your thoughts, and stop the habitual cycle of negative thinking.

Also, don't be a grumbler or complainer. Remember, the Lord hates that. Even if you are grumbling and complaining in your mind for God sees everything. He sees the grumbling and complaining in our thoughts. Your mind and your brain are two different parts of your body. When you become born again, you now have two persons living inside of you; you and the Lord Jesus Christ. Jesus operates in your subconscious, which is your brain. That's why He can see everything you think and feel. Nothing about you is hidden in His sight. Then, you are still there, of course, (smile). The you operates in your mind, (which is emotions, will and intellect). The place where you think and feel. So, He see's the grumbling and complaining. He made the children of Israel walk around in circles in the wilderness for 40 years because of it. You do not want to be covering the same ground year after year as if going around in circles. It is time for a change;

change your thinking. The children of Israel's mumbling, grumbling and complaining were negative thinking that turned into spoken words because what you think is what you speak. God hated that and would not and could not bless them. Do you think God likes it now? Of course not, and He yearns to bless you.

This has been a great deliverance and revelation for me because I am/was famous for watching my confession. But my thinking was wacky. I would not say anything but faith filled, positive things a large percentage of the time. Then at other times when I caught myself, I would stop and begin to speak faith again. But I was not allowing my thinking to line up with my confession. In my mind, I complained about the bills. I complained about; this one was doing this, and that one wasn't doing that; when I should have been thinking on the Word of God.

You can change your world by what you think. Wasn't there a famous book out called, "Think and Grow Rich?" Think about that. The Bible says, *Whatsoever things are true, whatsoever things are honest, whatsoever things are just, whatsoever things are pure, whatsoever things are lovely, whatsoever things are of good report, if there be any virtue, if there be any praise, **think** on these things (Phil 4:8).* So each time some negative thought or negative circumstances come your way, you have the power to think differently. Use that power.

Feelings

I often think about how down through the years we have been deceived by the devil with certain phrases. The phrase could be true but could also be looked at in another way. One is, we don't walk by our feelings but by faith. Well, that's true. We should not walk by our negative feelings. But the part I am talking about is, if you were like me, I completely threw feelings out the box. I did not realize how important it is/was to take those feelings and monitor them. My feelings are helpful in assisting me to monitor the 30 to 60,000 thoughts that I have a day. I monitor my feelings by lining them up with the Word of God, when they are contrary to scripture. This is how we create the God kind of life in our lives that the Lord Jesus died for us to have. You will have good feelings and you will have bad feelings. Each one empowers you. Bad feelings empower you to think or do bad things, so that you create bad things in your life. Good feelings, good thoughts empower you to do good and you create good things in your life. This, also, is the law of sowing and reaping. Just stop and ask yourself today, "How am I feeling right now"? If it is contrary to what the Word of God says, change it. Begin right now to feel prosperous, feel loved and feel healthy. Think on beautiful things and see don't good, beautiful things come to you. If something is in your life today, you drew it to you with prolonged thoughts.

__Guard Your Heart__

Also, you should guard your heart. Now, how did I jump from mind to heart? Well, nothing can get into your heart without it first coming into your mind. And what gets into your heart is a feeling that originated from a thought. That 's why the Lord said, *Guard your heart with all diligence, for out of it flows the issues of life (Prov. 4:23)* and to guard your heart, you must guard your thinking. Let's look at the word "issues". What does it mean? Issue means "giving out", or "to come forth", or "the result of an action". Alright, what comes forth or flows out of your heart? What is the "giving out" of your heart? Thoughts, the things we think about. What is the result of an action that comes forth from your heart? Happiness comes from your heart. Joy comes from your heart. Pain, concern, love, falling in love, anger, frustration, bitterness, goodness, and mercy all these things flow or comes forth from your heart and is the result of an action (your thinking).

For example, John says, I love Susie so much. I can't live without her. If I can't have her, nobody will. How did that get into John's heart? By his thinking. It started with a thought. It started in his mind and got into his heart. We can live without a human being. But we can't live the kind of life we were created to live without God. Happiness, joy, pain, concern, love, etc., are all things you think; things you feel. I think I'm happy, so I feel happy. I think I am in love, so I feel love. That's why one should guard their heart so that the right things can flow out of it.

Chapter IV
Your Belief and Attitude

*A*ll *things are possible unto thee if you believe (Mark 14:36).* To believe something, you must think about it first, right. Well, take thought to the next level, and think on it, think on it, and think on it, until it becomes a belief; a knowing. I know that I am healed. To know that you are healed, you are thinking healing, right. In other words, meditate on it, mediate on it and mediate on it until it becomes a knowing in your spirit or shall we say in your thoughts, in your mind. Thoughts are spirit. You cannot see a thought. If you are meditating on something, you are thinking, right?

As God-like creatures, we are to hold on to the thoughts of what we want. We are to let it be clear in our minds. That's how we develop and empower our belief system. Then the greatest power ever known (which is God in us) sees us believing Him and He brings that thing to pass in our lives.

Your attitude determines your altitude. I know you heard that one before. Well, how does one get an attitude, (be it a good attitude or a bad attitude)? By something they were thinking. How does one start to believe something? It starts with a thought.

I went to the store the other day to take some end tables back. They were still in the boxes. They were heavy and I landed them on the check out counter. I knocked the little gadget on the floor that you use to scan the price of merchandise. I told the security guard, I knock the merchandise scanner down. He looked at me as if to say, so what, I'm not picking it up. I thought to myself, Lord that's why we are in the state we are in now. It's our attitude, our thinking. Your attitude is what you think. You become the sum total of what you think. Here's another example. I went into the office the other day and I asked a guy, Hey, what happening? He said, very proudly, "very little". I thought to myself, Lord we shall have just what we say which is just what we are thinking. Why not say, life is phenomenal. Life is glorious. Life is just simply beautiful and how are you? You create your world by what you say. What you say is what you are thinking. Then too, if you are confessing the right things, make sure your thinking lines up with your confession.

If you see it in your mind, you will have it in your life. If you can see it in your mind, you can possess it. Think about what you want. Make it your dominant thought, and you will bring it into your life. Say to yourself over and over and over again. I am a winner, I am an over comer. I am blessed and highly favored. I am genius in my own right. I am a brilliant-minded person. I possess the supernatural ability of Almighty God to do all things thru Christ who strengthens me. I am empowered by the Most High God. I am in my wealthy place. I am in my wealthy place. I know I said many of these things before. But they are worth repeating. I must continually stir up your pure minds.

You are more powerful than anything in this world because of the One who lives inside of you. The power of your thoughts and your confession can reach cities, countries, and nations. It changes lives. It delivers nations. It can change your life. Use that power, which is your mind, your thinking and change worlds. Change your world.

Chapter V
How Does One Think Abundance?

L et's define the word "abundance". A great quantity of valuable material, possessions, resources, or riches. Let's define the word "wealthy", It means prosperous or affluent. Think of Jesus, isn't He invaluable, prosperous, affluent, wealthy and the more. To think wealth, health and prosperity, it is a continuous process. It is something you must do forever because our external environment is often unduly negative. One of the first words we hear is no. And so those negative influences continue throughout our life time. What we need to hear more of are, "praises of things done well".

I asked the Lord, how does one think "abundance" and "wealth" all the time? God walked me through this book even as I was typing it. What do I mean by that? He let me live the example as I was writing this book. I work with the mentally challenged and physical disabled. Several clients developed the flu, Type A. Different ones in the office were concerned about it spreading and rightful so. Well on that Thursday afternoon I started to feel weak, tired, aching, chills and shivering, even though it was about 75 degrees in March. I first rebuked the sickness. It acted as if it wanted to stay. I began to quote scriptures. It still acted like it wanted to stay. Then in my mind, I began say to myself over and over again I am healed. I am healed. I am healed. I said it about 25 times. A short time later, the symptoms were gone while others were beginning to feel bad and going home sick. They were confessing and focusing on the symptoms or thinking on, I don't want to get sick. I just went to the lounge off by myself because I knew within I was feeling bad. I didn't want to say anything to anyone. I did not want to give voice to it. From that experience, I learned how to think wealth. You think wealth, health and abundance all day long, by saying it over and over and over and over in your mind. Say things like God will increase me more and more. God will increase me more and more. Use this technique when something begins to attack your mind or your body. Right then I was beginning to be attacked with a sickness. So, instead of dwelling on feeling bad, I dwelt on (by saying in my mind) I am healed over and over and over again. Think on the Word of God. The Word is *health and healing to all our flesh, (Prov. 4:22)* and wealth, too. So you have to get into the Word and meditate on it day and night. Meditating is just simply thinking; quiet, deep, passionate thinking. Don't make it complicated. Get in the Word and let the Word get in you. *If you mediate in My Word both day and night and observe to do all that there is therein, then you will make your own way prosperous and have good success (Joshua 1:8).* How can you take it to the next level of, observing to do, if you don't first think about something. Let's paraphrase it. If you think on my word both day and night and observe to do all that you think about, day and night, you will make your own way prosperous which means you will draw to yourself good success. It really is another way of saying, be passionate about what you think about and what you think about you will do and become. Do it with your whole heart and you will make your own way prosperous and good success will come to you.

Material Wealth

To attract money, you must focus on wealth. (I can hear Christians screaming right here, focus on wealth). Nine times out of ten you are focused on not having enough. So, why not change your focus and focus on wealth. Don't focus on not having enough. Focus on abundance, plenty, and having more than enough. *Psalms 115:13 & 14 says, The Lord will bless those that fear Him, both small and great. He shall increase you more and more, you and your children.* Think increase, more and more increase, not only for me but for my children also.

Write scriptures on prosperity; speak to yourself all day about prosperity. I have more than enough. I live in abundance. I live in prosperity. I am in my wealthy place. I have more than enough money. Money cometh to me on a continuous basis. I have everything I need and feel happy about it. You must rejoice in the Lord always and again, I say rejoice. Let God's glory upon your countenance radiate out to the world, joy and happiness and excitement. It is the quickest way to bring anything to you. What you focus on is what you get. Focus on thoughts of wealth. God will move people, circumstances, elements, and events to bring that wealth to you. Think prosperous, affluent thoughts. Your wealth is waiting for you to bring it from the invisible to the visible, from the supernatural to the natural.

Think your way to prosperity. Think wealth. Think wealth. Think wealth. So as man thinketh so is he. Think money comes easy and frequently. Don't forget to pay your tithes and give your offerings. God says, when you do that He will rebuke the devourer for your sake and pour you out blessings you won't have room enough to receive. Give to charity type causes. Be a giver. It's more blessed to give than receive. Then, of course, in your giving you will receive.

Make room to receive your desires/dreams. Take action. Do something signifying you believe you have received. Go look at that dream house, drive that dream car, etc.

As you proceed along this line, God will give you a plan of action. Take steps to work diligently on that plan of action with His supernatural ability empowering you. Then see the hand of God manifest your dreams/desires right before your eyes.

Chapter VI
You Must Have Joy

The scripture says, *I give you joy unspeakable and full of glory (I Peter 1:8)*. That's powerful. *Joy unspeakable.* The dictionary says, it means joy inexpressible. Excitement and enthusiasm is a force that touches lives. Celebrate good feelings. Be excited about life, your goals, your dreams, and your aspirations. Think on things that give you joy. How do you feel when you celebrate Jesus? How did you feel when you first became born again and accepted Jesus into your life? You had so much joy. It is impossible to praise the Lord with all your heart and feel sad, too. Your feelings will eventually line up with your praise. This is re-directing your thoughts. I will praise the Lord instead of focusing on what tries to make me sad, despondent, and depressed. The key to creating your fantastic life is, **you must to have joy.** I was listening to a doctor and he said, one key to losing weight is you have to feel good. He said, because when you feel bad, it sends a chemical reaction to your brain, your mind, that makes you want to eat something. So even in losing weight, it has to do with what you think and feel.

The Lord declares it as saying, *Count it all **joy** when you fall into divers temptations, knowing this that the trying of your faith, (the trying of your thoughts, your feelings) worketh patience. And let patience have her perfect work that you may be perfect and entire, wanting and lacking nothing.* How will you be perfect and entire in wanting and lacking nothing? Because, through your faith (through controlling your thoughts and feelings) and through your rejoicing, you are exhibiting an attitude I already have what I requested. You are exhibiting an attitude that there is no lack. You are exhibiting an attitude that I am delivered; my prayer has been answered. Therefore, it has to come to pass. You have to keep rejoicing even in the midst of your faith being tried as you are waiting. You have to keep your joy. I call it having peace of mind; confident assurance that He who said it, will hasten to bring it to pass. That's all we want anyway is to feel good and feeling good brings peace of mind. Or, let's put it another way. How do you feel when you have peace of mind? Good, right. Be aware of when you are feeling good. These are empowering moments. Right then you are powerfully drawing more good into your life. What if, in your feelings, God is communicating to you how you are thinking. What if the Holy Spirit is putting a check in your spirit to tell you to line your feelings up with the Word of God, because they are fleshly now. They are negative now. They are faithless, now. Suppose the Lord is saying, change our thinking now, by using our feelings as a prompter.

The next time you are feeling bad or having negative emotions, listen to the feedback you are getting from the Holy Spirit. At that moment, you are blocking good things from coming to you because you are not joyful. The Holy Spirit is saying, start confessing faith filled thoughts/scriptures and bring that joy back alive again. Satan won't be able to steal your goods if he can't steal your joy. Things will try and come, but don't, "lose your focus", or "don't be distracted".

It's important that you keep your joy, because the joy of the Lord is your strength. This joy puts your ministering angels on assignment drawing more joyful things to you.

Think on the joy you would have when you get that particular thing you are thinking about. Make that joy alive and real in you by rejoicing. Rejoice always and again I say rejoice. Thinking the right thing causes you to say the right thing. Say to yourself, this is the day the Lord has made, I will rejoice and be glad in it. Think things like, I rejoice in the Lord always. I delight myself in you, Lord. Happy am I am because my God is my Lord. Father, thank you for loving me and rejoicing over me with joy. Thank you for redeeming me. Father, I come with singing and everlasting joy is upon my head. I obtain joy and gladness and sorrow and sighing flee away. Father, the spirit of rejoicing, joy and laughter is my heritage. I praise you Father with joyful lips. I make melody to you, Lord in my heart. My happy heart is good medicine. My cheerful mind works healing. My countenance radiates the joy of the Lord. I receive so that my joy, delight, gladness is full, complete and overflowing. The joy of the Lord is my strength. My God is the Lord and I am strong in Him.

It did not say that you would not have afflictions or trials. The Bible says, *many afflictions are the righteous but the Lord delivers us out of them all (Psalm 34:19).* Don't dwell/ think on the affliction(s). Think and dwell on the fact that you are delivered. The Bible says, *In this world, you shall have tribulation, but be of good cheer for I have overcome the world.* Don't think on the tribulation, but think of the fact that your God, your King, your Lord, Your Savior has overcome the world, and He said, be cheerful. The Lord Jesus said, *as I have overcome and sat on the right hand of the Father, you shall overcome and sat on the right hand of me.* The Bible clearly tells us what we are to think on, and meditate on. Think on your having the victory in all areas of your life in Jesus name. Praising the Lord always works in bringing and keeping you joyful. Going to church, getting into the presence of God, at home, in your car are also key ways of having and keeping that cheerful state of being.

Here's an example of how the devil might try to steal your joy. Suppose, the Lord told you to not to eat anything after 7 p.m. every night. Then one night, you miss it. You know what happens, your flesh tells you, go get something else to eat. Then you eat something else. Then your flesh tells you again, you have already blew it two times now. So you might as well eat something else and repent later. Then you might go get something else to eat especially if you are a person that have challenges with your eating habits and the Lord is working on your disciplining yourself in this area. Flesh wants you to continue that downward cycle and now lose your joy because you have sinned. Flesh/devil wants you to feel(think) condemned or condemnation because you blew it. Yes, we should feel sorry for our sins and any acts of disobedience. *But there is no condemnation for those who walk not after the flesh but after the Spirit (Romans 8:1).* You don't have to continually feel condemned after you have asked for forgiveness. Walk in the Spirit. How do you walk in the Spirit? By thinking the right things. Repent now, and start over. Start your train of thought over. Say to yourself, I have been forgiven. Then don't eat anymore the rest of the night.

You choose to go back and forth to the kitchen and eat all night or you choose not to go back and forth to the refrigerator all night. What were you thinking that has caused this behavior? Is there anxiety going on, worry or upset? Change your thinking and get your joy back. This example applies to any area where you might have made a wrong move. Repent, turn away from the thing and go on.

Chapter VII
Loving Thoughts

L oving thoughts is what makes this concept work so powerfully. If you do everything in love, engulf every thought in love, your life will be transformed.

The Bible says, *owe no man nothing but to love him (Romans 13:8)*. Think loving thoughts toward yourself and others and that is what you will manifest.

The Book of Jude tells us, *"But, beloved, (even the word beloved is a loving word). But beloved, building up yourselves on your most holy faith, praying in the Holy Ghost. Keep yourselves in the love of God, looking for the mercy of our Lord Jesus Christ unto eternal life (Jude 1:20).* Praying in tongues helps us to walk in love. The greater degree in which you feel love, the greater the power of God you will feel harnessing from and to you. You must love God. You must love yourself. I'm not talking about being conceited. But have a healthy respect for yourself and then for others. Love the Lord God with all your heart, with all your strength and with all your might and with every fiber and tissue of your bones. Then, love your neighbor as yourself. You must know that you are important and the next person is as important as you are.

Everything we want, whatever it may be is and should be motivated by love. It is to experience the feelings of love in having Jesus, in having family, friends, things, youthfulness, money, career, health, the right person in our lives, etc. To receive the things we desire, we must radiate love and those things will appear immediately. It's all about loving God and loving people.

This is where the Body of Christ has missed it. We are getting prophesied to, hands laid on; getting in special lines with our $1,000.00 seed, our $100 seed, but not operating in love. God is not going to give us the millions with hatred in our hearts; won't speak to each other, having respecter of person(s). I don't like this one or that one. You can't be trusted with millions with that kind of disposition. This is where the devil is deceiving us. Then we get upset with God because our breakthrough didn't come to pass after we planted that seed. Suppose the one you don't like, God wants you to sow a seed into their lives. It would be difficult to do unless you let the love of God be perfected in your heart. No love in your heart can also cause sickness and dis-ease as well as hold up your millions. Oh, you will be blessed, but it will only be a mercy drop here and there. Don't you want the floodgate of blessings? I know you do. Your motivation must be pure love.

Let's talk about loving yourself. Well, the devil had me thinking that to think on me was sin. To love yourself, you have to think about yourself, sometime at least, right. Well, of course, we don't want to idolize ourselves. But it's okay to think you are fantastic. Jesus thought you were so fantastic that He shed His Blood for you on the Cross. So it's okay to love yourself. You do that by focusing on the real you. The you inside. The you that is made in the image of God. Focus on God's presence in you. Take a moment and be still. As you focus on His presence in you, He will begin to reveal Himself to you. It is a feeling of pure love, joy and Holiness. His presence is the perfection in you.

Don't look at yourself with critical eyes, but focus on who God says you are. Look at yourself in the mirror. Tell yourself, I will praise the Lord, because the Lord says, *I am fearfully and wonderfully made (Psalms 139:14)*. Think about the presence within and all your imperfections will dissolve, because He did not come to condemn you. Perfection manifests when you focus on God, His presence and His love.

Love

What is love, anyway? Love is patient. Love is kind. Love is never envious, never boils over with jealousy. Love is not boastful or vainglorious. Love does not display itself haughtily. Love is not rude and unmannerly. Love does not act unbecomingly. Love does not insist on its own rights or its own way. Love is not self-seeking, touchy, fretful or resentful. Love takes no account of an evil done and pays no attention to a suffered wrong. Love does not rejoice at injustice and unrighteousness but rejoices when right and truth prevails. God's love causes one to be able to bear up under anything and everything that comes. Love believes the best of others. Love endures everything without weakening. God's love in us never fails, which causes us to never fail. This doesn't say that you will never have the opportunity to get jealous or you will never be unkind again. But when the opportunity presents itself to do that you can immediately *bring your thoughts into captivity unto the obedience of Jesus Christ (II Cor. 10:5).* If you are unkind, you can immediately repent and start right back to thinking and acting like you are the righteousness of God in Christ Jesus and begin to walk in love again.

Here are some confessions that you could say to yourself regarding the love of God operating in your thought life. The love of God is perfected in my heart by the Holy Spirit in the name of Jesus. Perfect love in my heart has cast off fear. I walk in the God kind of love and the God kind of faith. By the way, what is the God kind of faith? *If you have the faith as a grain of a mustard seed, you can say to the mountain, be thou removed and cast into the sea and it shall go into yonder places* (if you don't doubt). The God kind of faith, is faith that is unmovable, unshakable and does not wavier. It's the kind of faith that moves mountains. It knows that without a shadow of a doubt that mountain has gone into a yonder place. Think on the love of God in me approves things that are excellent. I plant seeds of love. My Father prepares hearts ahead of time to receive this love. Seeds of love flowing out of my heart are producing God's love in the hearts to which they are given. I flow in the love of God. People are blessed by that love. I flow in the wisdom of God. People are blessed by that wisdom. I find favor, compassion and loving-kindness with others. The love of God cannot be separated from my life because I am rooted deeply in that love, founded securely on that love and God is on my side.

The Magnificence of God's Glory in this World

This is a magnificent world the Lord has given us. God's Glory shines throughout the whole earth and that Glory is upon you for He said it is your re-reward. God thru this world is bringing good things to you now. God is conspiring good things for you this very moment.

The Lord God said, *I have plans for you, to give you a future and an expected end (Jer 29:11).* That wonderful expected end, of course, is to reign with Him forever and ever and ever. But also to live life to the fullest here, too. We have the best of both worlds. A life made to enjoy here and over there. Think, my Father, *withholds no good thing from me because I walk up right before Him.* You have a covenant right to have good things come to you. Good things are your birthright. Jesus said, *I came to give you life and life more abundantly*. When you became born again and made Jesus your Lord and Savior, a good life became your birthright.

Think to yourself, life is easy. Life is good. All good things come to me now. Begin to think this all day long. Right now you are discovering that it is God's heartbeat to bless you and to manifest Himself through you. So, welcome to the world of **"the world is waiting for the manifestation of the sons of God"** (Romans 8:19). Our manifestations of the Glory of God upon our lives have begun, because we have taken control of our thought life, which controls our destiny and we are living the Success Filled Living paradigm. Everything that comes into my experience, I summons from this moment onward by my persistent thoughts.

Chapter VIII
Three Steps

The Lord is always looking at and listening to everything you, think and speak. Nothing is hidden from His sight. God says, ask me anything in my Son's name (Jesus) and I will do it. In order for you to ask for it, you had to think it first.

Step One

The first step is to ask. Ask and it shall be given unto you. Let God know what you want. God must want to respond to your petition(s) or He would not have told you to ask. Amen. What do you really want? Sit down and write it down on a piece of paper. The scripture says, *Write the vision and make it plain upon tablets that he may run that readeth it. For the vision is for an appointed time, but at the end it shall speak and not lie, thou it tarry, wait for it, for it will surely come to pass, it will not tarry. (Habakkuk 2:23).* Don't write the vision in the future tense; God is going to bless me. God is going to make me a millionaire. God is going to heal me. No, make it present tense. Lord, I thank you that my tithes are thus and so every month. I thank you that I am healed in Jesus name. I thank you that every artery, tissue, fiber of my body functions in the perfection God created it to function and I forbid any malfunctioning in Jesus name. I thank you that I am making how ever, much money you want to make in 6 months, one year, next 5 years. I thank you Father that I have all sufficiency in all things. I thank you that my children have graduated from college, tuition paid, doing well and serving you. Be clear about what you want. Don't be double minded. The Bible says, you will not receive anything from the Lord if you believe today and doubt tomorrow. There are no limits to what you can ask for. Make it a habit to ask.

Since I have been controlling my thoughts, the Lord orders and direct my steps even more. It has caused me to spend more time with Him, getting to know His voice and His ways. I find that when I need an answer, I ask Him and

He answers me or gives me direction. This also helps one to never be stumped on anything again for God's Wisdom will cause you to be on top of every circumstance or situation that may arise in your life. In the process, one is becoming so close to the Lord. Just ask. You only need to ask once. Then begin to thank Him for its fulfillment.

Step Two

The second step is to believe. Believe that it is already yours. *When you pray, believe you have received and you shall have whatsoever you prayed for.* You must know that what you ask for was yours the moment you made your request. You must have unshakeable faith; knowing that you have received. Know God, the El Shaddai has shifted the entire elements of heaven and earth to bring that thing to you. Claim the things you want. Visualize your having it. Don't try to figure out how it is going to happen. You just keep the faith that it has happened. When you are trying to work it out, you are sending a thought of "lack of faith", that you don't believe you already have it. When you don't see it when you feel you should see it, don't get disappointed or doubled minded. Turn that doubt into mountain moving faith. (I know that I have it" kind of faith"). Wait for Him.

Third Step

The third step is to receive. Begin to feel wonderful about it. Be happy. Go home, to the office, to church with joy. When you exhibit joy, you are putting yourself in a level of faith that you have received. See yourself with those things and feel the "unspeakable joy", you would have as if it had already manifested. The Lord says, *I give you joy "unspeakable" and full of "glory"*. As I mentioned earlier, the definition of, "unspeakable", is inexpressible joy. Joy beyond description, inexpressible happiness. Then look at the word "glory". Glory means great honor, praise, adoration, splendor, a height of achievement, enjoyment, prosperity, and a highly praiseworthy asset. God has sent his Son Jesus to give you great honor, praise and He adores you. Adore Him in return. He wants you to abide in the splendor of His glory, have enjoyment, and prosperity. Feel the joy. Feel the feeling of living in that dream house, driving that dream car, seeing souls come to Jesus, having your bank account look like you want it to look. You have to have the corresponding feeling, underneath your prayer that says, I got what I prayed for **now.** And that is your constant thinking. All you have to do to receive is feel good about it. That really, is operating in faith. If someone came up to you right now and gave you a million dollars, how would you feel? FEEL IT.

But Satan wants to intercept by causing an event to come to make you feel sad or despondent. For instance, you are expecting the check in the mail. You called the company, got someone on the phone that says your paperwork cannot be found. But you talk to someone the other day. They said everything was okay. Don't get despondent. Keep your joy and keep saying in your mind I have the check in my hand. The check is here. See yourself going to the bank to deposit the check. Visualize actions in motion, getting the car, driving to the bank, standing in line and depositing the check. The check will arrive if you don't doubt and if you don't believe the adverse circumstances around you.

You are believing God you are healed. A pain shoots up your arm. You want to doubt. But don't. Let your mind think and thank healing. Put on music, pray and rebuke the pain. Call someone else to agree with you. But do something to let your mind know that you will not wavier; that you have what you say in spite of. Even go to sleep if necessary. Sleep helps to change your mindset, too.

Just begin to say, I receive good in my life now. I receive my abundance now. I receive my wealthy, healthy place now.

When you feel as though you have it now and that feeling is so real. You shall receive what you ask for.

You will be shown the way by God. You might get an inspired idea that you have to act upon. Remember *Habakkuk 2:23 said, that he may run that readeth it (there is work involved)*. It might appear by someone bringing something to you to do. Thru your doing that you get what you believed for. It will require action on your part, so be open. You know that it is your answer, because you will feel so joyous, so alive, looks like heaven has opened up for you and you could do that thing all day. Empowerment is what you are looking for in bringing your dreams to pass. Because work that is empowered seems like work that it done so easily and without a struggle. It will be the anointing of receiving in action, propelling you to that thing you have desired. When there is empowerment, the task is effortless and it feels wonderful. You will know that it is God answering you because it won't be hard or a struggle. You will be moving in God's anointing; the flow of His supernatural power. Then you will look back and see how God answered your prayer by bringing you what you wanted, or by bringing what you wanted to you. Don't delay, don't be slothful. Don't doubt. When the opportunity comes, when the supernatural strength of God is there, when that intuitive feeling from within is there, act. That's your job. That's all you have to do. Trust your instincts. It's God inspiring you. It's God communicating with you on the receiving end. When you have that instinctive feeling, follow it. You will find that God is supernaturally moving you to receive what you asked for. Have you heard of the saying, "when the student is ready, the teacher will appear. Everything you need to get the job done will appear; be it money, person, book, lawyer, etc. Pay attention to what comes into your life. Because as you hold the visualization, the thought of what you want, you are going to draw it to you by things and those things are going to be drawn to you.

Your Physical Body

Let's look at your body, the temple of the Holy Spirit. If you want to lose weight or believing God for a healing, are you looking at yourself fat? Are you looking at yourself sick? Are you thinking fat thoughts? Are you thinking, "I am sick". You must begin to see yourself thin. You must begin to see yourself healed. See yourself at your desired weight. Get some pictures of you when you were thin. Or get some pictures of someone else that is thin and visualize that in your mind. Don't think about losing weight, because you create what you think about. You attract back continually have to lose weight. Think perfect weight. Think perfect thoughts and the result will be perfect weight. Go to the bathroom. Look yourself in the mirror. Say, Hi, Jane Doe. You are the temple of the Holy Spirit. God says that anyone who defiles the temple, He will destroy. Defiling the temple can mean in many ways, but right now we are talking about appetite, your eating habits. Say, I love you Jane Doe. (You must make sure you love yourself). I want the best for you. I want you to have good health and live a long time. So we are changing some things right now as I speak to you Jane Doe. You weigh a 130 pounds in the name of Jesus. You are trim and attractive as unto the Lord. You are no longer deceived by deceitful foods and dainties. You eat and you eat until you are satisfied, until hunger is appeased and then you stop. I chew my food slowly. You eat only as much as is sufficient for you. You love drinking 8 to 10 glasses of water a day. Water is delicious, um, um. (smile). Water is good for the temple of the Holy Spirit. Water is the cheapest fat burner on the market. It flushes poisons and toxins out of my body. I love fresh fruits, salads and vegetables. I love to exercise, or take a brisk walk. Say it many times a day. But the key is to look yourself in the mirror and talk to yourself.

Buy yourself a scale. Write your desired weight on a piece of paper and tape it over the glass part of the scale. Weigh yourself many times a day (every time you pass by that scale) for several months looking at yourself at that desired weight. Program your mind at yourself desired weight and watch and see doesn't it materialize. I found that when I got on the scale and it said 180 lbs, I ate just enough food to keep me at 180 lbs and/or to gain more. Chew your food slowly, enjoying every bite. I grew up feeling I had to eat every bite off my plate because otherwise I am wasting food. Think how many hungry children would love to have that food. So what I do now is, I put smaller portions on my plate. Ask God what is a perfect weight for you. Think that weight and think thin and thin you will become. Think fat and fat you will stay. Stop thinking that food is responsible for making you fat. Because as long as you think that, you create that. Act as if you are at that weight. Buy clothes at that weight. See how happy you would be at that weight. Praise and admire people who are at their desired weight. If and when you see overweight people, don't focus on them. Keep picturing thin thoughts always. Keep picturing always and saying, I am at my ideal weight. And then last but not least, when you feel the strength to stay out of the kitchen, to not to eat, to stop when hunger is appease, you must flow with that strength. When you feel that empowerment, you must let it work for you and obey its instructions. If you mess up, repent and start over. I know how you feel. I have been there. It is like this little nagging something is sitting on your shoulder, whispering in your ear, eat, eat, eat. It's like something is driving you to the refrigerator, to the fast food carry out. Do what the Word says, resist the devil and he will flee. You resist the devil by speaking the Word of God to him. Satan, I rebuke you in the Name of Jesus. I am not hungry. You are suggesting to my mind to eat when I do not need any more food. Quote scriptures. Man shall not live by bread alone but by every Word that proceeded out of the mouth of God doeth man live. So, get thee behind me Satan. Then turn your mind to Jesus and worship Him and thank Him for using the devil to remind you to worship and praise God. Turn it into communion and special time the Lord. You continue to do that on a really basis. Satan will leave you along for a long time because he hates it when you worship and praise God. Use this same concept for your healing also. This, too, will cause you to have a new, fresh, lovely, and closer relationship with the Lord.

Time Frame

Time is on your side. Don't be concerned about how long it will take to manifest your dreams/desires. It takes no time to manifest what you want. God is God and He answered you when you first prayed. The time delay comes from your getting to the place of believing, knowing and feeling you already have what you ask for. Since the writing of this book, I have noticed things come to me in a few moments, in a few hours, the next day. Some things I have a time line on like 30 days, 6 months, one year, etc.

As I was driving home from work the other night, I was crossing a bridge. I looked over the city with its beautiful lights. I thought to myself, this whole world is mine. It was such an awesome feeling. When you get to that feeling, you feel no lack. You feel like everything is already yours, already there for you; **like you already have it all**. That's when powerful manifestations begin. Every thing in this world is yours, because *you are an heir with God and joint-heir with Jesus Christ.* He told us in the Word. *Everything in this world belongs to Me, therefore, everything in this world belongs to you because you are Mine. If thou canst believe, all things are possible.* You must learn how not to be rushed and in a hurry. The Lord says *"be anxious for nothing"*. But *in everything with thanksgiving, make your supplication and prayer known to God.* Being anxious means, being rushed, being fearful, and being in a hurry. Let the peace of God rule your heart as you create your world by your thoughts, your prayers. Know God has heard your supplication and not only heard but answered, too. Meditate, think to yourself, I have more than enough time to do all the things I have been destined to do and I receive all the things I have been destined to receive. This will cause you to rest and not be anxious.

God does everything with zero effort. The trees and flowers do not strain to grow. Think about a baby in its mother's womb. It does not strain to grow fingernails, toes, hair and develops into human form. It's a miracle indeed. It's all about what's going on in your mind. The Word says, *don't be double-minded, for a double minded man is unstable in all His ways and do not think He will receive anything from the Lord.* You provide the feelings of having it now. It will manifest. That's why you hear men and women of God talking about us constantly, get in the Spirit or be prayed up. There is a place in God you can get where you have no doubt. That's why things are always manifesting for them. In your thinking, you can get into a place where you have no doubt and that's why monitoring your feelings/thoughts are so important. Another way of looking at it is, *praying without ceasing*. I use to wonder how could one pray without ceasing. Well, now I know. You will definitely be in an attitude of prayer all the time because thoughts never stop coming, be it good or bad. So, monitor your feelings, that way you will monitor your thoughts. That is a good way to keep praying; to be in a mode of prayer all the time.

Chapter IX
Prayer

Well, let's not leave prayer out. Yes, prayer. You could really call what we have been doing up to this point, different types of prayer. Here is another type. Speak the word over your desires/your thoughts. Bind and loose in the name of Jesus any thoughts that does not line up with the Word of God. You have the authority to bind and loose *and whatever you bind on earth shall be bond in heaven. And whatever you loose on earth shall be loosed in heaven.*

There are powers behind your thoughts and feelings, be it good or bad. The negative powers can influence someone to kill, steal and indulge in all manner of destructive activities.

These powers can influence Christians to gossip, to slander people, or to bear grudges against each other. It can cause you to eat too much and cause you not to fast or participate in church activities. These powers can cause you to be lackadaisical when it comes to the things of God. It tries to convince us to spend more time in front of the television rather than reading our Bibles. These powers can draw Christians away from paying their tithes or only pay a portion of their tithes and, not the right amount. These powers can work through pastors from different congregations or the same congregation, members alike trying to keep the Body of Christ from working together. All these things start with our thought life. Go behind the scenes (in other words, pray in tongues) and bind the strongman behind any activity that would try to mitigate, abort or come against your destiny and your families' destiny and your church. Curse to the root anything that may be trying to hold up the progress of your church, hold up your miracle, hold up your finances, hold up the deliverances of your children, hold up your career, ministries, your dream house, dream car, your wealthy place, etc. Quote scriptures regarding the situation(s) and then do spiritual warfare by praying in tongues. Stop and begin to praise God for great things in your life and in the lives of others. Take dominion over your mindset and don't let the devil have a foothold anymore by taking control of your thoughts. Say to yourself continually, I have the mind of Christ. I have mind of Christ. I have the mind of Christ. Well, what is the mind of Christ? The Word of God. So, get in the Word and let the Word of God get in you. Confess, I hold the thoughts and purposes of God's heart. Know that Satan has been defeated by the work of the Cross through our Lord and Savior Jesus Christ. Don't give him any victory by giving over to him your thought life. **Take it back. Take it back.**

You have an enemy. The enemy is spiritual. He operates thru your mind. You have a God who is not your enemy. God is spiritual. God operates through your mind. Mind your thoughts and create that phenomenal life God has for you.

Chapter X
Thanksgiving

O ne way to change your thinking is to start being grateful. Remember, the song, Count Your Blessings. Count your blessings, name them one by one. Well, that song still works, instead of focusing on things to complain about, be thankful.

Begin to praise God. It brings more good things into your life. The Lord is to always be worshipped and praised and adored. It keeps you in a positive, joyful state of mind, which causes positive, good things to come to you.

Be grateful for what you already have and see more come to you. Many people keep their lives in poverty and ill-will by complaining about the state they are in and being ungrateful.

Not being thankful, blocks anything good from coming your way. Suppose you want a new car. You must be thankful for the one you have or thankful that you have the strength to catch the bus or walk. Instead of getting up every day, saying this old beat up car. It needs to go the junkyard. Or, every day I have to walk three blocks in the cold. The buses are never on time. I hate riding the bus. Guess what you are creating. It becomes more and more miserable to catch the bus or to drive that car. The daily practice of thanksgiving gives way by which your new car, wealth, good health and abundance comes. Lord, I thank you for this car that I have. I thank you that I can walk. I thank you that this city has a metro system where we can get to and fro. There is something in life I know that you are and can be thankful for.

Each morning before you get out bed, make it a habit to feel the feelings of thanksgiving in advance for the glorious day in the Lord you will have today. David said, I will bless the Lord at all times. His praises shall continually be in my mouth. I will bless Him in the morning, in the noonday and in the midnight hour. Thanksgiving or praise shall I say, speeds up your wealthy place.

Chapter XI
Visualization & Being Still before the Lord

Visualize what you want and dwell on the end result. Create a picture of something you want in your mind. Start with something small to start increasing your faith. Watch and see doesn't it come to pass. Begin to expect great things and you will build your life in advance.

Visualize yourself in your dream house, singing before thousands of people if singing is what you want to do. See yourself laying hands on the sick, and seeing them recover, etc. If you can see it, you can achieve it. Then feel that dream, that thing, that desire so real in your life. It becomes so real in your life till you feel like you don't need it anymore because you have the feeling of "I have it already". You see the manifestation of it already. Then you shall see the manifestation in reality thereafter if you don't doubt. Put yourself in feeling of I have that car. Not, I wish I could get the car. Or, I'm gonna get the car. That's the future. To often, I hear ministers say, God is gonna bless you. God is gonna heal you. That's in the future. Your confessions must be in the present, in the now. I thank God that by His stripes I am healed. I thank God that I am bless and highly favored. The blessings of Abraham are mine now. I have the car now and feel the feeling of, "I have the car now". Go to the dealership and sit in that dream car if necessary.

The power to move worlds lives inside of you. Tonight before you go to sleep, visualize how you want your day to go the next day, believe, receive and see the manifestation of it. Feel the joy of that great day. Know that everyday the Lord gives you adds new purpose and meaning. When doubt comes or events occur to distract you, re-direct your thoughts.

The Secret Place

Let's talk about the secret place. *He that dwelleth in the secret place of the Most High shall abide under the shadow of the Almighty (Psalms 91:1)*. Let me ask you a question. What does that scripture mean? What is the secret place? The secret place is your mind, your imagination. You can use your mind, your imagination and go anywhere in the world. Why not use it as a secret place for you and God, and abide in and under the shadow of the Almighty. How do you go there? Remember, I said earlier, you now have two of you living inside of you, the Lord Jesus Christ via the Holy Spirit and yourself. The Lord operates in your subconscious (your brain) and you operate in your conscious (your mind, will and intellect).

Remember the show that used to come on called, "Laugh In". This actress came on sitting in a BIG rocking chair. They made her real small and she would be rocking in the chair and talking. Visualize the Lord Jesus sitting a GREAT, BIG rocking chair. You are sitting in His lap. You are talking to your Daddy, your Heavenly Father, your Protector, your Shield, and your Comforter, telling Him anything you want. You can close your eyes at home or you can be sitting at your desk typing and still do this exercise, because it is in your imagination. In your mind, say, Lord, I love you. Lord, I praise you. Lord, I thank you for being supreme in my life. You can say, Daddy, I thank you for helping me to realize a lot was given up for me; the shed blood of Jesus Christ to live life more abundantly. So, I am going to take you at your Word and declare my wealthy place now. I am in my wealthy place now. I thank you that I am living in abundance right now. I thank you that I am prosperous right now. I thank you that checks are coming to me in the mail right now. I thank you that men are pouring into my bosom blessings that I don't have room enough to receive right now because I give, therefore, it is given back to me. I thank you and I love you with all my heart, all my soul and all my mind and every fiber of my being. I thank you for healing, Lord and that every tissue, fiber, artery of my body functions in the perfection it was created to function and I forbid any malfunctioning right now in Jesus Name. I thank you Lord for putting into my path three souls every day that I tell about the love of Jesus. I thank you that I am your witness in the earth. This is how you go into the secret place. You can use any picture you want; Jesus with outstretched arms, simply waiting for you to come into His presence and talk with Him. Whatever it takes to make the secret place real to you, go there.

Being Still Before the Lord

Let's talk about being still before the Lord; another way of getting closer to God. Lie down in the morning and at night or sit in your lounging chair. Start by taking 5 - 10 deep breaths. I say the, ah, ah, ah, sound because I am a speaker so I am getting my voice exercises in as well. The correct way to breath is take a deep breath thru your nose, pushing your stomach out at the same time. Hold for a few seconds. Then push the air out thru your nose and pull your stomach in. If you are doing the, ah, ah, ah, sound then you push the air out thru your mouth because your mouth is open while doing the ah, ah, ah, sounds. It may be hard at first because you may not be use to breathing like this. But this is the correct way to breath. Statistics say, that many dis-eases could possibly be alleviated if we would stop and do this about 3 times a day, learning how to properly bring oxygen into our lungs. Then after those 5 - 10 deep breaths, you say to yourself, be still and know that I am God. Be still and know that I am God. Be still and know that I am your God about 5 times. Then do 5 – 10 more breathing techniques. Then say this. Thank you Lord for my being my God, my King, my Lord, my Savior, my all and all. Thank you for your love, your strength, your joy and your crown. I worship you for being the Great God that you are. You are the Sustainer of my life and the Keeper of my soul. Then you talk with the Lord saying His Word back to Him or whatever phrases you want that praises and adores Him. Let Him know that this is not a monologue but a dialogue. Ask God if He has anything He would like to say to you. Then be quiet. Allow the Lord to speak to you. Keep pen and paper nearby because sometimes the Lord gives you instructions, or gives you a Word. So be ready. Then begin to see yourself as the Word says you are, in your wealthy place, healed, prosperous, more than enough, having all sufficiency in all areas of your life, in your dream house, driving your dream car, children saved, your career, ministry flourishing, etc. Do this every day, at night before bed, in the morning before going to work, during your prayer time, or when you standing in a long bank line. You can take these deep breaths standing in the bank line, or grocery line without doing the, ah, ah, ah, sounds, of course, and still "be still before the Lord".

This is the secret place that causes us to draw nigh to God, become more intimately acquainted with Him and know Him even the more. Drawing nigh to God simply means the closer we get to God, the closer God will be to us.

When you meditate, don't allow your mind to be blank. You should be worshipping God, praising Him, thanking Him and/or quoting scriptures back to Him in your mind, bringing your petitions before Him, praying about whatever He brings to you to pray about and then allow Him to speak/ talk to you. He will make you into a brand new woman or man if you do this every day and night or at least once every day. The more the merrier.

Suppose you are thinking about your current state of affairs. If it is not what you desire for your life, change your thinking by being still before the Lord. As you do this at night, let the Holy Spirit bring back to you all the things that He was not pleased with that day. When I lay down at night, the Lord always bring back to my remembrance my day. For example, you offended Susie today, so you must get that straight. I didn't like the way you did thus and so. Then, the Lord might show me a better way. That is your opportunity to change your thinking, repent if need be, and visualize good events appearing next time around.

Let God, the creator of the universe grant you your every command. He says, I *will withhold no good thing from him who walketh upright before Me. Ask the Father in Jesus Name, whatever you will and it shall be done so that your joy may be full, complete and overflowing.* You must be alert and on guard to the power of right thinking. Let that secret place be a place where you re-think what you are thinking if need be.

How do you wake up in the morning? Do you wake up expecting the children to misbehave, the spouse to be a jerk, the boss a pain in the neck? Guess what? That's what you will get. Start your day by beginning to think what beautiful, mannerable, respectful, obedient children you have. Start thanking God for that. That is what will begin to manifest . Your children will begin to behave and then God will show you as a parent and leader how to reinforce those good behaviors, by praise, acknowledgements, loving rewards, etc. Start thinking of good qualities about your spouse, your boss. Focus on that and create more of that.

Chapter XII
Be Strong in the Lord

The scriptures say, finally my brethren, be strong in the Lord and in the power of His might. Where do you want to be strong? In your mind, thinking strong or faith-filled, positive thoughts. *Put on the whole armor of God that you may be able to stand against the wiles of the devil. For we do not wrestle against flesh and blood, but against principalities, again powers, against the rulers of the darkness of this age, spiritual wickedness in the heavenly places. (Where do you wrestle, (in your mind, in your thought life). Don't we say that the mind is the battle ground. Therefore take up the whole armor of God that you may be able to withstand in the evil day, and having done all, to stand. Stand therefore,*

having girded your waist with truth (where do you want to put the truth (in your mind/your thoughts), having put on the breastplate of righteousness. (Why do you want on the breastplate of righteousness? To guard your heart. Why do you want to guard your heart? Remember, earlier, we said, out of your heart flows the issues of life, which are your feelings, affections that influence you. You get feelings and affections first from your thinking a thought; And having shod your feet with the preparation of the Gospel of peace, (where do you want the Gospel of peace to be? (In your mind/thoughts) which will keep your heart. Above all, take the shield of faith with which you will be able to quench the fiery darts of the wicked one. Where will you quench the fiery darts? (In your mind/thoughts). And take the helmet of salvation and sword of the Spirit, which is the word of God. Put it in your heart, which will also guard your thinking.

You work for a company and with that company you have benefits, health insurance, dental, life insurance and even retirement after so many years of service. Well, with serving the Lord comes benefits. The benefits of health insurance, (divine health). The benefit of provision, (promising that He would take care of us, meet our every need). He already knew and knows what we have need of. Life insurance, (eternal life) and that He would go with us all the way to the end of the world. That is not to say, you are not to have natural life and health insurance that covers your family in this life. But you have covenant rights and privileges as a son/daughter of the Most High God. **Become more aware of who God is and who He says you are in HIM.** God says, I am God and besides me there is no other God. I am the greatest power ever known. Greater than any demon, devil, principality, ruler of darkness, spiritual wickedness in high places, any nuclear bomb, atomic energy, or person, things and I have chosen to live on the inside of you. You are my children, my royal priest hood, my holy nation, my peculiar people, called forth out of the world to show forth my praises. You are more than a conqueror, you are my ambassadors. Live like kings and priest in the earth.

The Heavenly Place

The Lord said to you, *I have made it possible for you to sit in heavenly places in me in Christ Jesus.* Where is that heavenly PLACE? Your body is still right here on the earth. That heavenly place is in your mind, your imagination. You can go heaven and back, in your mind, in your imagination, in your secret place. In your mind, you can continually orchestrate and cause your thoughts to think joy, peace, love, abundance, perfect health and think all things working together for your good. Think great things over your children, your job, career, ministry, think living in your dream house, living in your wealthy place, driving your dream car, being that desired weight, traveling all over the word ministering for Jesus, etc. What the mind can conceive, it can achieve. It sounds like some heavy thinking going on here.

Fellowship

Fellowship, that is what God has been desiring from us all these many years. He desires our fellowship, our companionship, our love and to be included in our daily lives no matter how small or great. There is nothing he won't do for us. Look at your children in the natural. If you have a healthy, genuine love for your children, there is nothing you won't do for them. How much more the Heavenly Father? If you start doing what I am talking about in this book, your life will never be the same. You will begin to experience a closeness and a fellowship with the Lord that is so sweet.

Begin to practice the presence of the Lord with you always. Say to yourself, I know that the Lord is with me 24 hours a day so I am mindful of what I think, mindful of what I do, mindful of what I say, mindful of where I go, and mindful of how I carry myself.

Here are several key areas to be mindful of His presence in your life: your time, your talents, tithes, witnessing and Bible study. You will find God's blessings flooding into your life like a torrent if you give God time by studying your Bible, and reading good, life giving books. I shared already different ways to pray without ceasing and staying in communion with the Lord. Make it a daily habit to spend time being still before the Lord everyday getting your instructions from on High. Get the events of your life in advance through your meditations and prayers. Give God your talents. Let them be used to bless others. Let them be used for Kingdom building, for profiting withal. Tithes, you must give God 10% of all of your earnings or else you will operate under a curse. You will still be a child of God but you won't be experiencing the Success Filled Life He wants you to have. You will get mercy drops of blessings here and there. The Bible says *to bring the tithes and offerings into the storehouse so that there may be meat in God's house and prove Me, saith the Lord. See don't I pour you out a blessing that you won't have room enough to receive. One other translation said, see won't I cause your investments, your stock, etc., to bring forth a harvest and an increase.* Prove God. Witnessing, tell someone about Jesus everyday. People love to talk about the weather. So thank the Lord for the weather when someone comments on the day. Tell someone of something special the Lord did for you that you were not expecting or about answered prayers. Make witnessing a high priority in your life.

Finally Thoughts

Ask the Lord to dispatch ministering angels (which are flames of fire) to bring in your wealth. They are ministering angels sent forth to minister to the heirs of salvation. That's you. Put them on assignment. They are waiting. Let them be sent forth in everything you do and everywhere you go by thinking and speaking the way you want things to go in advance. Then, look for the elements of heaven to be propelled in your life in many ways: a phone call, a check in the mail, an ideal, a magazine article, announcement, clicking on the business channel, a miracle, a certain food to eat that is good for a particular ailment, a contract, etc.

The greatest power ever known lives down on the inside of you. It is the same power that raised Jesus Christ from the dead. That power has given you dominion over the fowls of the air, the beast of the field, the fish of the sea and every creeping thing. That power spoke through a prophet and told the sun to stand still. What sun do you need to stand still in your life for your miracle to come to pass, for your monies to mainifest, for that deal to come through, your dream house, tuition for your child, etc? How much and what can you think on/believe God for and **don't doubt. <u>ASK</u>, <u>BELIEVE</u> and <u>RECEIVE</u>** . Then you will be creating your life on purpose and enjoying **<u>Success Filled Living</u>** everyday.

Confessions to Pray While Being Still Before the Lord

I worship You, Heavenly Father for keeping me safe and for You being my refuge.

I thank You for being my Master and letting me know that all good things come from You.

I thank You Heavenly Father that you alone are my inheritance, my cup of blessing.

I thank You Heavenly Father that You guard all that is mine and that the land You give me is a pleasant land. I worship You for such a wonderful inheritance.

I thank You Father for I know that You are always with me.

I bless Your Name because You guide me continually into all truth.

I thank You Lord for I will not be shaken because You are right by my side.

I thank You Heavenly Father that because of You my heart is filled with joy and my mouth shouts Your praises knowing I rest in Your safety and care.

I thank You Father because You continually shows me the way to life, granting me the joy of Your Presence and the pleasures of living with You forever.

I thank You Heavenly Father that because of You I am fortified as a secured wall.

I thank You Lord that Your protection is continually upon me and Your unfailing love and mercy is forever with me.

I worship You Heavenly Father at Your throne, Eternal High and Glorious Lord, the hope of all mankind.

I worship You Heavenly Father because You alone can save us and heal us, oh Lord.

I reverently worship You Heavenly Father because You search the heart. You examine all secret motives and gives all people their due rewards, according to what their actions deserve.

I thank You Heavenly Father that when we put our confidence and hope in You, we are like trees planted near riverbanks who roots grow deep into the waters. We are not bothered by drought or heat, our leaves stay green and keep right on producing delicious fruit.

I thank You Heavenly Father because You have taught us to wait upon Your Counsel and to never forget all that You have done for us.

I worship You and Praise You because the God of all gods rescues us from our enemies and redeems us from our foes.

I thank You Heavenly Father that I have entered into my promised land and I am eating of the pleasant land that You have given to me and my family.

I thank You Heavenly Father that You have given us long, full lives.

I worship You Heavenly Father for answering us and rescuing us with Your Mighty Power continually.

I worship You Heavenly Father because You grant us our heart's desire and fulfill Your plans for our lives.

I thank you Father that for poverty You have given me wealth, for sickness You have given me health and for death You have given me eternal life.

Lord, I want to thank You because You are my Shepherd and I do not want because Jesus was made poor that I through His poverty might have abundance. For He came that I might have life and have it more abundantly.

I thank you Lord that the Spirit of truth abideth in me and teaches me all things. He guides me into all truths. Therefore, I confess I have perfect knowledge of every situation and every circumstance that I come up against.

I am filled with the knowledge of the Lord's will in all wisdom and spiritual understanding.

I am increasing in the knowledge of God. I am strengthened with all might according to His glorious power.

The Lord takes pleasure in my prosperity. Abraham's blessings are mine.

These are just a few scriptures. You can take this so many ways by finding scriptures to pray. And, of course, I have continually said throughout the book, think, confess, medi-tate on your being in your wealthy, healthy, place.

Love you, in Jesus Name.

References:

Prayers that Availeth Much
Word Ministries, Inc.

Longing to be Loved
C. S. Lovett

Binding the Strong Man
ArchBishop Nicholas Duncan-Williams

LaVergne, TN USA
14 February 2011
216548LV00002B/99/A